OHIO STATE FOOTBALL ★TRIVIA★

BILL BORST

Quinlan Press
Boston

To the members of my "fan club," Judy, Mark, Michelle and Matthew, who left me alone long enough to finish this book.

I would like to acknowledge the assistance and the guidance of Kevin Stevens of Quinlan Press and the staff of the OSU archives, especially Ann L. Guevin.

Known as the "Baseball Professor" for his college-accredited baseball history courses, Bill Borst is the author of nine books. He is the founder of the St. Louis Browns Fan Club, which has been written about in the *New York Times*, the *Los Angeles Times* and *Sports Illustrated*. Borst is a weekly host on WGNU radio and a monthly commentator for KMOX radio in St. Louis. A native New Yorker, he lives in St. Louis with his wife and three children.

Contents

Woody Hayes

"He's indomitable in defeat, insufferable in victory!"

1. What was the dual significance of Woody's date of birth?

2. Where did Woody play college ball?

3. What position did he play?

4. What is his wife's name?

5. What branch of the service did Hayes join in 1941?

6. Did Woody have any children?

7. Where was his first football coaching position?

8. How many games did that team win his first season?

9. Where was his next position?

10. What was his first bowl appearance as a college coach?

11. What year did Woody first come to OSU?

12. Who was his predecessor?

13. How many seasons did Hayes coach at OSU?

14. What was his record?

15. How many times in his tenure did he beat Michigan?

16. How many National Championships did he win outright?

17. How many Big Ten championships did he win outright?

18. How many did he tie for the leadership?

19. Under what circumstances was Woody Hayes fired?

20. Who was the linebacker Woody hit?

21. What was the score of the game?

22. Who threw the pass that was intercepted?

23. According to Woody, what is the function of local announcers during an OSU broadcast?

24. Who was Woody's favorite politician?

25. What was Woody's favorite intellectual pastime?

26. What was his distinctive OSU headgear?

27. What often happened to this headgear?

28. Was it ever premeditated?

29. In 1972 whom did Woody make co-captain in opposition to the popular choice of the rest of his players?

30. What short phrase described Woody's approach to football offense?

31. What was the score of Woody's first OSU football game?

32. When did he lose his first OSU football game and who was the opponent?

33. What was Woody's record his first year at OSU?

34. What went wrong with his system the first year?

35. What was his record during his final season?

36. What was his best season as OSU coach?

37. What major change did Woody make in the OSU offensive alignment when he first came to OSU?

38. Whose college career did this hurt?

39. How did Woody use former Heisman Trophy winner, Vic Janowicz, in 1951?

40. What pet peeve of his got him in trouble?

41. What famous US General did Woody most admire?

42. Woody's 1955 quarterback had played which position the prior season?

43. Woody was the first OSU coach to win back-to-back conference championships since when?

44. Who was the greatest running back Woody Hayes ever coached?

45. Name four of Woody's big bruising fullback types.

46. How many losing seasons did Woody Hayes have at OSU?

47. What trait did Woody look for most in his quarterbacks?

48. Where was Woody's office on the OSU campus?

49. How many trips to Vietnam did Woody make during the war?

50. How would someone describe his politics?

51. Who was the only OSU Heisman Trophy winner who did not play for Woody?

52. How soon after the Gator Bowl in 1978 was Woody fired?

53. Name the title of the book written by Woody Hayes.

54. What was the score of Woody's first OSU-Michigan game?

55. What was the score of Woody's last OSU-Michigan game?

56. What were the most points a Woody Hayes team ever scored in a game?

57. What were the most points scored against a Woody Hayes OSU team?

58. What very successful Big Ten coach was Woody's assistant from 1958-63?

59. Who was Woody's first quarterback?

60. Who was the captain on that first team?

61. Who were the captains of Woody's last team?

62. Who was his last quarterback?

63. When was Woody's last win over Michigan?

64. When did Woody first beat Michigan?

65. What was his record against Michigan State?

66. Which opposing coach was his fiercest rival?

67. What was his record against Indiana?

68. What was his record against Iowa?

69. What was his record against Northwestern?

70. What was his record against Purdue?

71. What was his record against Illinois?

72. What was his record against Minnesota?

73. What was his record against Wisconsin?

74. What was the score of Woody's last win?

75. What did the OSU players do in 1952 after they tied Illinois 0-0?

76. What was Woody's most bizarre rule that the players revolted against?

77.   Why was it difficult to find a seat on two of the OSU buses on the way to and from the Michigan game in 1952?

78.   What happened to Woody's 1952 quarterback the next season?

79.   What was unusual about this switch?

80.   Who was Woody's quarterback in 1953?

81.   What were his stats that year?

82.   What position did Burton play in 1954?

83.   Who was the first of his big rushing fullbacks?

84.   Who had the best rushing average of the three members of Hopalong Cassady's 1955 backfield?

85.   Who were the great ends that Woody had on the 1954 team?

86.   Who was the coach of the Northwestern team that surprised Woody by a score of 21-0 in 1958?

87.   What post-game amenity did Hayes often refrain from?

88.   What was his shortest post-game press conference on record?

89.   What special act of self-flagellation did Woody engage in after seeing a bad play on the game film in 1962?

90.   Woody once referred to one of his players, "That Marcie . . . or however you say his name . . . could start for any other team in the country." Who was he talking about?

91.   What was Woody's record in the Rose Bowl?

92.   What was his overall Bowl record?

93.   What was his worst defeat?

94.   What was his biggest victory?

95.   In which year did Woody's bowl team threaten a "Mutiny"?

96.   What were their "demands"?

97.   What caused Woody to go berserk in the 1971 Michigan game?

98.   How many people saw Woody lose his temper in the 1971 Rose Bowl?

99.   To whom did Woody compare the editors of the OSU student newspaper in 1971?

100.   Which former president did Woody eulogize at the 1973 Rose Bowl luncheon?

101.   Who was the photographer that Woody assaulted during the 1973 Rose Bowl game?

102.   How many shutouts did OSU have under Woody Hayes?

103.   How many times were Woody's Buckeyes shut out during his tenure?

104.   Who eulogized Woody at his funeral?

Answers

1. He was born on St. Valentine's Day in 1913, the year OSU entered the Big Ten.

2. Denison University

3. Tackle

4. Anne Gross (in 1942)

5. The Navy

6. One son, Steven

7. Denison

8. Just one

9. Miami University (Ohio)

10. He beat Arizona State in the 1950 Salad Bowl.

11. 1951

12. Wes Fesler

13. 28 years, from 1951-1978

14. 205-61-10

15. 16-11-1

16. Five: 1954, 1957, 1961, 1968 and 1970

17. Seven

18. Six

19. He punched a Clemson player in the Gator Bowl in 1978.

20. Charlie Baumen

21. A 17-15 loss

22. Art Schlichter

23. To serve as the team's publicists

24. Richard M. Nixon

25. Reading military history

26. A black OSU baseball cap with a white "O" on it

27.　He often ripped it into pieces.

28.　Sometimes he cut it with a razor blade before the game, so it tore more easily.

29.　All-American, John Hicks

30.　"Three yards and a cloud of dust"

31.　Beat SMU 7-0

32.　Lost to Michigan State in his second game, 24-20

33.　4-3-2

34.　It was too complicated.

35.　7-4-1

36.　10-0 and a National Championship in 1968

37.　He went from the single wing to the split T.

38.　Heisman Trophy winner, Vic Janowicz

39.　He used Heisman winner Janowicz mainly as a decoy.

40.　He hated marching bands on soft turf—it hurt his running game.

41.　George Patton

42.　Frank Elwood had been an end.

43.   Since Dr. John Wilce in 1916-17

44.   Archie Griffin over Hopalong Cassady

45.   Bob White (1956), Bob Ferguson (1961), Jim Otis (1969) and John Brockington (1970)

46.   Two (1959, 1966)

47.   Intelligence

48.   2nd Floor of St. John's Arena

49.   Four

50.   Conservative to reactionary

51.   Les Horvath (1944)

52.   The next day

53.   *You Win With People* (1973)

54.   Lost 7-0

55.   Lost 14-3

56.   63 against Northwestern in 1978

57.   42 by UCLA in the 1972 Rose Bowl

58.   Bo Schembechler

59.   Tony Curcillo

60.   Bob Haid

61.   Ron Springs, Tim Vogler, Tom Cousineau and Byron Cato

62.   Art Schlichter

63.   1975 (21-14)

64.   1952 (27-70)

65.   9-7

66.   Forest Evashevski

67.   22-1-1

68.   20-5

69.   18-4

70.   10-4-1

71.   22-4-2

72.   11-1

73.   26-1-2

74.   21-18 over Indiana in 1978

75.   Locked him out of the dressing room

76.   No singing in the showers.

77.   Woody was all alone in the third bus.

78.   Became a linebacker

79.   He was the team's leading rusher.

80.   John Borton

81.   115/196—both school records to that point

82.   Linebacker

83.   Hubert Bobo

84.   Both Bobby Watkins and Bobo had 6.3 rushing marks to Cassady's 5.4.

85.   Dean Dugger and Dick Brubaker

86.   Ara Parseghian

87.   Handshaking

88.   One minute

89.   Ramming his school ring into his forehead until he drew blood

90.   Ron Maciejowski (1968-70)

91.   4-4

92.   5-6

93.   32-3 in 1963

94.   56-0 over Indiana in 1957

16

95.   1970 Rose Bowl

96.   A later curfew

97.   Michigan's Tom Darden's interception of an OSU pass

98.   106,000, plus millions at home watching on TV

99.   Vidkun Quisling, the Norwegian traitor in 1940

100.   Harry Truman

101.   Art Rogers of the *LA Times*

102.   41

103.   14

104.   Richard M. Nixon

The Heisman and Other Awards

"I always dreamed of winning the Heisman, but I never thought I would be good enough!"
—Archie Griffin

1. Who was the first Buckeye to win the Heisman?

2. Who is the only two-time winner of the Heisman in college football history?

3. Who was the first Buckeye to finish in the Top Ten in voting for the Heisman?

4. How many Heisman winners has Ohio State had?

5. Until Bo Jackson swung a bat for the Kan-

sas City Royals in 1987, who was the only Heisman winner to play major league baseball?

6. What professional teams did he play for?

7. What is the only school that has had more winners than Ohio State?

8. Actor William Boyd had what in common with Hopalong Cassady?

9. How many Buckeyes have been runners-up to Heisman winners?

10. In 1944 whom did the Buckeye Heisman winner beat out for the award?

11. Whom did OSU's Heisman winner beat out in 1950?

12. In 1955 the Heisman winner from OSU beat out which players who later starred in the NFL?

13. The OSU two-time winner edged out two players from the same school in successive years. Who were they?

14. How many OSU alumni are enshrined in the Pro Football Hall of Fame in Canton, Ohio?

15. Who is the only head coach who is enshrined in the Pro Football Hall of Fame?

16. Which Buckeye lineman won the first Vince Lombardi Award in 1970?

17. How many other Buckeyes have won this award?

18. Who was the first Buckeye to win the Outland Award, given to the best interior lineman since 1946?

19. Have any other Buckeyes won the Outland?

20. When and where was Les Horvath born?

21. Who were his coaches at OSU?

22. Where did OSU finish nationally when he won the Heisman?

23. Where was he in 1943?

24. Under what circumstances did he play during his Heisman year?

25. What was the highlight of his Heisman year?

26. What profession did he go into after graduation?

27. What are his pro stats?

28. What is Janowicz's middle name?

29. Where and when was he born?

30. Who was the man that most influenced Janowicz's decision to play college football instead of pro baseball?

31. Against whom did he have his greatest college game?

32. Is there anything he didn't do on the football field?

33. How many punts did he have blocked in the "Blizzard Bowl"?

34. What did Janowicz do after he won the Heisman?

35. What did Janowicz do after graduation?

36. What tragedy ended his pro career?

37. What baseball positions did he play?

38. What Big Ten great did he play against in the Big Leagues?

39. What was his major league batting average?

40. How many homers did he hit?

41. How many points did he score for the Skins in 1953?

42. How many were from touchdowns?

43. Who beat him out for the scoring title?

44. By what other nickname was he known?

45. What kind of a debut did Hoppy make in 1952?

46. According to Woody Hayes, what was the greatest play that Cassady ever made?

47. Why did Cassady play left-half and not right halfback?

48. What was his last home game like?

49. What future star with the Los Angeles Rams did Cassady make game-saving tackles on twice in the 1955 Rose Bowl?

50. Whom did Cassady edge out for the Male Athlete of the Year in 1955?

51. How many touchdowns did he score in the NFL?

52. How many seasons did Cassady rush for 1000 yards or more as a Buckeye?

53. In addition to the Heisman, what other major pro-season awards did Cassady receive?

54. Where does Griffin rank on the OSU All-Time Scoring List?

55. What did Archie Griffin's parents nickname him?

56.   What did his little league teammates call him?

57.   What did his OSU teammates call him?

58.   Griffin holds the record for the most consecutive 100-yard games. How many times in a row did he rush for 100 yards in a game?

59.   How many Rose Bowls did Griffin start in?

60.   What was OSU's record with Michigan during the Griffin years?

61.   What was OSU's record with Griffin on their team?

62.   How many games did OSU lose to Big Ten opponents during the Griffin years?

63.   Who was Archie Griffin's first quarterback?

64.   How many times was Griffin an All-American?

65.   How many times was he the OSU Co-Captain?

66.   How many of his brothers played major college ball?

67.   Did any of them play at OSU?

68.   What other Big Ten school did he intend to play for before Woody Hayes talked him out of attending?

69.   How did Archie Griffin debut at OSU?

70.   How about his next game?

71.   Who ended his streak of 100-yard games?

72.   Archie Griffin was picked on the second pick in the first round in the 1976 NFL Draft. Who was picked ahead of him?

73.   Which team drafted Griffin?

74.   How many pro seasons did he play?

75.   What positions did he play?

76.   What was the last football team Archie Griffin toiled for?

77.   Who is the only OSU assistant coach who made it to the Coaches' Hall of Fame?

78.   How many OSU coaches are in the Coaches' Hall of Fame?

79.   How many OSU football players are in the National Hall of Fame at Canton, Ohio?

80.   Who was the first OSU player to be named Scholar Athlete?

81.   Who was OSU's only three-time Scholar Athlete?

82.   Who was the first OSU player to win the Silver Football?

83.   Who was the last one to win it?

84.   How many Buckeyes have won the Silver Football?

85.   Who was the only two-time winner?

86.   One OSU Heisman winner failed to win it the year he won the Heisman Trophy. Who was he?

87.   Who edged him out for the Silver Football?

88.   Who are the only quarterbacks to have won the Silver Football?

89.   Which years did OSU players win the award three years running?

90.   Who was the first Buckeye lineman to win both the Lombardi and the Outland Trophy?

91.   Which Buckeye came within a few votes of being the only college football player to win the Outland, Lombardi and Heisman Trophies?

92.   Who were OSU's three All-Americans in 1958?

93.   Who were the first OSU players to be named consensus All-Americans?

Answers

1. Les Horvath in 1944

2. Archie Griffin

3. Gene Fekette in 1942

4. Five

5. Vic Janowicz in 1950

6. The Pittsburgh Pirates and the Washington Redskins

7. Notre Dame, now with seven

8. He portrayed the cowboy hero, "Hopalong Cassidy" on TV.

9. Four-Cassady in 1954, Bob Ferguson in 1962, Paul Warfield in 1963 and Art Schlichter in 1979

10. "Mr. Inside and Mr. Outside" themselves, Doc Blanchard and Glen Davis of Army

11. Kyle Rote of SMU

12. Cassady beat both Earl Morrell of Michigan State and linebacker Sam Huff of West Virginia for the award.

13. Steve Bartkowski in 1974 and Chuck Muncie

14. Two—Jim Parker and Paul Warfield

15. Paul Brown who coached in 1944

16. Middle guard Jim Stillwagon

17. Just offensive tackle John Hicks in 1973 and Chris Spielman in 1987

18. Jim Parker won it in 1956.

19. Stillwagon in 1970, and Hicks in 1973

20. South Bend, Indiana on September 12, 1921

21. Francis Schmidt, Paul Brown and Carroll Widdoes

22. Second, behind Army

23. He was in the US Army Dentistry Program at OSU.

24. His studies gave him an extra year of football eligibility.

25. His two touchdowns in a come-from-behind victory over Michigan

26. He played for the Los Angeles Rams and the Cleveland Browns.

27. He rushed 58 times for 221 yards, and one touchdown. He caught nine passes for 142 yards and one touchdown.

28. Felix

29. Elyria, Ohio on February 26, 1930

30. John Galbreath, a wealthy OSU patron and sports owner

31. Against Iowa, he ran for two touchdowns, passed for four and kicked ten PAT's, as OSU romped to an 83-21 victory in 1950.

32. Everything but lead the cheers, he was a consummate triple-threat back who ran, passed, kicked and caught

33. Four out of his 21 punts

34. He flunked out of school; he reapplied and was readmitted.

35. Went into the army

36. An auto accident

37. Catcher and third baseman

38. Paul Giel, who starred at Minnesota and pitched for the NY Giants

39. .214

40. Two in 1953

41. 88 points

42. Seven (four rushing and three receiving)

43. Doak Walker of the Detroit Lions

44. Red

45. Three touchdowns against Indiana

46. An 88-yard touchdown run after an interception against Wisconsin in 1954

47. So he could follow All-American Jim Parker who opened huge holes from his left guard position.

48. Three touchdowns against Iowa

49. Jon Arnett

50. Heavyweight Champion, Rocky Marciano

51. Six

52. None—his best was 958 in 1955.

53. The Maxwell Trophy, the Walter Camp Trophy and the AP Player of the Year

54. Sixth with 222 points

55. Butterball

56. Tank

57. Duckfoot

58. Thirty-one

59. Four (1972-75)

60. 3-0-1

61. 40-5-1

62. Twice (to Michigan State both times)

63. Greg Hare

64. Three times (1973-75)

65. Twice (1974-75)

66. All six of his brothers

67. Ray and Duncan

68. Northwestern

69. Woody saved him for the last two minutes of the Iowa game.

70. He rushed for 239 yards against North Carolina, scoring his first touchdown in OSU's 29-14 win over the Tarheels.

71. In 1975, Michigan held him to just 46 yards.

72. Leroy Selmon of Oklahoma was drafted first by Tampa Bay.

73. Cincinnati Bengals

74. Eight

75. Running back and wide receiver

76. Jacksonville Bulls of the USFL in 1985

77. Ernest Godfrey (1929-61)

78. Four: John Wilce, Homer Jones, Francis Schmidt and Woody Hayes

79. Thirteen

80. Quarterback John Borton in 1952

81. Dave Foley (1966-68)

82. Wes Fesler (1930)

83. Keith Byars (1984)

84. Eleven

85. Archie Griffin (1973-75)

86. Griffin (1975)

87. Cornelius Greene

88. Greene (1975); Art Schlichter (1981)

89. 1973-75 with Griffin and Greene

90. Jim Stillwagon in 1970

91. John Hicks (1973)

92. Jim Marshall, Jim Houston and Bob White

93. Chic Harley and Bob Karch (1916)

Big Games and Great Players

"Harmon of Michigan and Scott of Ohio State are good—probably great, but they can't class with Chic Harley."
                    —Former A.D. L.W. St. John's of OSU

1. If a book were written about all the men who played for OSU, what might the title be?

2. Who was the greatest player in OSU's first fifty years of play?

3. How many times was he an All-American?

4. How many career points did he have?

5. How long was this the school record?

6. Who broke most of his OSU records?

7. How many games did he fail to score in during his OSU career?

8. What position did he play?

9. What interrupted his OSU career?

10. What was the outcome of his final game for OSU?

11. What major league baseball team made an offer for his baseball services?

12. What track record did Harley hold at OSU?

13. What was his wife's name?

14. What affliction did he later suffer from?

15. During the thirties, what OSU College Hall of Famer, a lineman, was from Greece?

16. Who is the only OSU football player to be featured on one of *Life Magazine*'s two-thousand covers?

17. Ironically, three of OSU's greatest running backs were born in the same city. Name that city.

18. What was the "greatest game ever played" and what was the score?

19. Who was the OSU quarterback in that game?

20.   Which OSU player quickly went from the game's hero to the goat?

21.   Who was the first Buckeye to intercept three passes on opening day?

22.   What OSU back led the nation in scoring in 1972?

23.   Who was the first college football player to be named TSN's "Man of the Year"?

24.   How many losing seasons has OSU had?

25.   What was OSU's best season?

26.   What was OSU's worst season?

27.   When was their last losing season?

28.   Who was the great pro kicker who played the line for the Buckeyes in the forties?

29.   What OSU lineman, who would later star in the pros, scored both touchdowns in a 14-14 tie with Purdue in 1958?

30.   What former OSU quarterback, who switched to all-purpose back in the pros, was pressed into duty as a quarterback, complete with basic plays on his wristband, for the Baltimore Colts in the Championship Game in 1965?

31.   When OSU lost to Wisconsin in 1942, what was the nickname given to that day?

32. Which team edged out the 9-0 OSU team for the mythical National Championship in 1944?

33. What caused OSU to be known as a "graveyard for coaches" in the thirties and forties?

34. Who was the MVP in the Big Ten in 1941?

35. OSU had three All-Americans on its 1942 line. Who were they?

36. Tony James set a conference rushing record in 1942. What was it?

37. What was unusual about Woody Hayes's placekicker in 1942?

38. What pile-driving fullback at OSU later starred with St. Louis in the NFL?

39. What OSU alumnus ended Darrell Stingley's career and nearly his life with a vicious hit in the 1978 Exhibition Game?

40. What other OSU fullback was the star of the 1969 Super Bowl?

41. How long was Keith Byars' longest kick-off return?

42. Who was the only punter in OSU history to be named an All-American?

43. Name the football captains of the 1987 team.

44. Who were the captains of the 1970 team?

45. Who was the captain in the last year that OSU had just one field leader?

46. Who were the first co-captains since 1943?

47. Who were the first co-captains in OSU history?

48. Who was the first two-time captain in OSU history?

49. In which season did OSU have the most captains?

50. When did OSU last play the same team twice in a season?

51. Since 1947 what were the fewest points scored to lead the team in that category?

52. Who was the last regular season quarterback who failed to pass for 1000 yards?

53. Who was the first quarterback in OSU history to pass for more than 1000 yards?

54. Who was the first 100-point scorer in OSU history?

55. Who was the first rusher to surpass 1000 yards in OSU history?

56. When was the last time that a receiver failed to catch ten passes in a single season?

57. What future New York Met right-hander played fullback for Woody Hayes?

58. Who took his starting job as fullback from him in 1957?

59. Who was the star in OSU's come-from-behind victory against the Hawkeyes in 1957?

60. Who was the one-two backfield punch of the 1960 Buckeyes?

61. Name the members of the 1961 Buckeye backfield.

62. Who were the Buckeye co-captains in 1963?

63. What was the highlight of the 1962 season?

64. What was the passing combo of the 1963 Buckeyes?

65. What was the only highlight of the 1966 season?

66. What has been described as "the Golden Age" of OSU football?

67. Who was the quarterback on those teams?

68. Who was his back-up?

69. Name the rest of the backfield.

70. What potentially great OSU player was on the bench for two of those seasons?

71.   What was the team's composite record?

72.   To whom were the team's only losses?

73.   Which team scored the most points on those OSU teams?

74.   Who was the hardest hitter on those teams?

75.   What was the score of Rex Kern's last game against Michigan?

76.   Who replaced Rex Kern at quarterback in 1971?

77.   How long was Rex Kern's longest run from scrimmage?

78.   Who were the first freshmen to play under the change in freshman eligibility rules in 1972?

79.   How long was Archie Griffin's longest run from scrimmage?

80.   How long was Paul Warfield's longest run from scrimmage?

81.   Who was the Illinois quarterback who threw for 621 yards against OSU one afternoon and still lost the game?

82.   How many touchdowns did OSU give up in the air that day?

83. Who was the OSU quarterback and how many touchdown passes did he throw that day?

84. What terrible mental affliction later affected this OSU quarterback?

85. Who was the first black quarterback at OSU?

86. Whom did the latter beat out for the job?

87. How many passes did OSU starting quarterback attempt in the Michigan game in 1973?

88. Who threw OSU's only passes in that game?

89. What happened on his first attempt?

90. What OSU alumnus wrote the book *They Call Me Assassin*?

91. How many times did Archie Griffin lead the Buckeyes in scoring?

92. Which former Buckeye played in two Super Bowls for the Miami Dolphins in the seventies?

93. Who was a Rhodes Scholar from the 1985 team?

94. Who was Tom Tupa's back-up at quarterback in 1987?

95. How far was Tom Tupa's longest punt?

96. Which OSU player once lost to Mike Tyson in a Golden Gloves fight?

97. Which team in the World Football League did he toil for?

98. What was his last pro team?

99. What great OSU athlete was drafted by the NFL, yet he never played a down for OSU?

Answers

1. *From Abbott to Zizakovic*

2. Chic Harley

3. Three times

4. 201

5. From 1919-55

6. Hopalong Cassady

7. Just his last game against Illinois

8. He was a triple-threat player, running, kicking and passing.

9. World War I; Harley joined the Army Air Corps

10.   Lost 9-7 to Illinois

11.   St. Louis Browns

12.   The 50-yard dash

13.   He never married.

14.   Mental illness

15.   Gus Zarnas, 1935-37

16.   Paul Sarringhaus on October 22, 1945. Number 88 had just returned to school from the service and scored three touchdowns against Missouri.

17.   Chic Harley, Hopalong Cassady and Archie Griffin were all born in Columbus, Ohio.

18.   OSU lost to Notre Dame in 1935, 18-13.

19.   Stan Picura

20.   Dick Beltz who kicked the extra point, only to fumble and then get beaten deep on a pass play

21.   Craig Cassady (1975)

22. Champ Henson with 20 touchdowns and 120 points

23. Archie Griffin

24. Eleven

25. 1954 or 1968, both teams were National Champs and won Rose Bowls that year.

26. 1898 (1-7-1)

27. 1966

28. Lou Groza

29. Jim Marshall

30. Tom Matte

31. "Bad water game"

32. Army

33. Inability to beat Michigan

34. Jack Graf

35. Bob Shaw, Charlie Csuri and Lindell Houston

36. Rushed for 11.8 yards in twenty carries

37. He was left-footed.

38. Jim Otis

39. Jack Tatum

40. Matt Snell

41. A 99-yard touchdown against Pittsburgh in the 1984 Fiesta Bowl

42. Tom Skaldany (1974-76)

43. Eric Kumerow, Chris Spielman, William White and Tom Tupa

44. Rex Kern, Jan White and Jim Stillwagon

45. Bernie Skvarka (1952)

46. Bob Joslin and George Jacobs

47. Jesse Jones and Paul Lincoln in 1890

48. Dick Ellis, 1891-92

49. Six in 1982

50. OSU defeated UCLA twice in 1982.

51. Three players scored just twelve points each in 1947.

52. Jim Pacenta in 1976 with just 404

53. John Borton with 1555 in 1952

54. Jim Otis with 102 in 1968

55. Otis with 1027 in 1969

56. Fred Pagac in 1972

57. Galen Cisco

58. Bob White

59. White

60. Tom Matte at quarterback and Bob Ferguson at fullback

61. Don Unverferth at quarterback, Bob Rein and Tom Barrington at halfback and Bill Sander at fullback

62. Matt Snell and Ormonde Ricketts

63. A 28-0 rout of Michigan

64. Unverferth to Paul Warfield

65. A narrow defeat to Michigan, 11-8

66. OSU's 1968-70 teams

67. Rex Kern

68. Ron Maciejowski

69. Leo Hayden, Jim Otis and Larry Zelina

70. John Brockington sat while Otis played.

71. 27-2

72. Lost to 24-12 to Michigan in 1969 and 27-17 to Stanford in the 1971 Rose Bowl

73. Illinois scored 29 in a loss to OSU in 1970.

74. Jack Tatum

75. Won 20-9

76. Don Lamka

77. A 76-yard touchdown against Illinois in 1970

78. Archie Griffin and Brian Baschnagel in 1972

79. A 75-yard touchdown run against Washington State in 1974

80. A 75-yard touchdown run in 1962 against Illinois

81. Dave Wilson of Illinois in 1980 in a 49-42 loss to OSU

82. Six

83. Art Schlicter threw for four touchdowns.

84. He was a compulsive gambler.

85. Cornelius Greene

86. Senior Greg Hare

87.   None

88.   Hare

89.   It was intercepted.

90.   Jack Tatum

91.   He never led OSU in scoring.

92.   Paul Warfield

93.   Mike Lanese

94.   Greg Frey

95.   75 yards against Illinois in 1986

96.   Paul Warfield

97.   The Memphis Southmen in 1975

98.   The Cleveland Browns in 1976

99.   John Havlicek of the Boston Celtics was drafted by the Cleveland Browns. It was rumored that he could throw a football sixty yards.

Bowl Games

"We just beat the best *team in the country!"*
—Quarterback Jim Plunkett of Stanford after his team upset the Buckeyes 27-17 in the 1971 Rose Bowl.

1. How many bowl games has OSU played in ?

2. What is their bowl game record?

3. How many times has OSU been shut out in a bowl?

4. How many times has OSU shut out its opponents?

5. How many points has OSU scored in its bowl appearances? a. Between 200-300, b. 301-400 c. 401-500 d. Over 500

Bowl Games—Questions

6. How many have they allowed? a. Between 200-300 b. 301-400 c. 401-500 d. Over 500

7. What were the most points ever scored by an OSU team in a bowl?

8. What were the most points they allowed in a bowl game?

9. How many Rose Bowl appearances has OSU made?

10. What is their record?

11. In what year did OSU play in its first Rose Bowl?

12. Whom did they play and what was the score?

13. When was their last appearance in the Rose Bowl and what was the score?

14. What is the only team not from a California school that OSU has played in the Rose Bowl?

15. How many times has OSU appeared in the Orange Bowl in Miami?

16. How many appearances has OSU made in the Sugar Bowl?

17. Who was their opponent and what was the score?

18. Has OSU ever appeared in the Liberty Bowl in Memphis?

19. Who did they play and what was the score?

20. Which was the least prestigious bowl OSU has played in?

21. Who did they play and what was the score?

22. Which were the only years that OSU played in two different bowl games?

23. What is the only bowl, outside of the Rose Bowl, that OSU has played in more than once?

24. Which state did both of their opponents come from in this bowl and what were the final scores of these games?

25. What is the only team, other than a Pac Ten team, that OSU has played more than once in the bowl games?

26. Which bowl games were they and what were the scores?

27. Has OSU ever played in a Cotton Bowl?

28. Whom did they play and what was the score?

29. Under what circumstances did OSU receive its invitation to the Rose Bowl in 1973?

30. How did OSU do in the 1973 Rose Bowl?

31. Who kicked the winning field goal for OSU in the 1949 Rose Bowl?

32. Which Big Ten team played in the Cotton Bowl before OSU?

33. Who kicked the winning field goal for OSU in the 1958 Rose Bowl?

34. How many yards did Archie Griffin gain in the 1973 Rose Bowl?

35. Who was the USC star of that game?

36. Who scored the winning two-point conversion to beat OSU in the Rose Bowl?

37. Who was the MVP of the 1984 Fiesta Bowl?

38. Who was the leading OSU rusher in the 1980 Rose Bowl?

39. Who was the leading receiver for the Buckeyes?

40. Who was the Buckeyes' leading receiver in the 1980 Fiesta Bowl?

41. Who was the leading rusher?

42. Who was OSU's leading rusher in the 1982 Holiday Bowl?

43.   Who was their leading pass receiver in this game?

44.   Who was the leading OSU rusher in the 1984 Fiesta Bowl?

45.   Who was the leading receiver for OSU in the 1985 Rose Bowl?

46.   Who was the leading rusher for OSU in the Rose Bowl in 1985?

47.   Who was the leading rusher for OSU in the 1985 Citrus Bowl?

48.   Who was the leading receiver for OSU in the 1985 Citrus Bowl?

49.   Which Big Ten Conference team played in all five major bowls prior to OSU?

50.   Who kicked the longest field goal in Rose Bowl history?

Answers

1. Twenty-one

2. 11-10

3. Just once, their first bowl game with USC, 28-0

4. Never!

5. c. 421

6. c. 420

7. 42 against USC in the 1974 Rose Bowl

8. 42 by UCLA in the 1973 Rose Bowl

9. Twelve

10. 5-7

11. 1921

12. Lost 28-0 to the University of California

13. They lost in 1985 to USC, 20-17.

14. Oregon in 1958

15. Once in 1977

16. Just one—in 1978

17. Lost to Alabama 35-6

18. Just once—in 1981

19. Beat Navy 31-28

20. The Citrus Bowl in 1985

21. They beat Brigham Young University 10-7.

22. 1980 and 1985

23. The Fiesta Bowl in 1980 and 1984

24. The "Keystone State" Pennsylvania; OSU lost to Penn State in 1980 (31-19) and beat Pitt (28-23) in 1984.

25. BYU in the Holiday Bowl in 1982 and the Citrus Bowl in 1985

26. They beat BYU both times, 47-17 in the Holiday Bowl and 10-7 in the Citrus Bowl.

27. Yes, in 1987

28. They beat Texas A&M 28-12.

29. After the famous 10-10 tie, the Big Ten voted 6-4 in favor of sending OSU to the Rose Bowl, mainly on the strength of the injury to Michigan University quarterback, Dennis Franklin.

30. USC massacred them 42-17.

31. Jim Hague

32. OSU was the first in 1987.

33. Don Sutherin

34. 95 yards in twenty carries

35. Sam "the Bam" Cunningham of USC

36. Thad Jemison

37. Jemison with 8-131 and one touchdown

38. Calvin Murray with 18-73

39. Gary Williams 3-131

40. Douglas Donley with 5-122-2 touchdowns

41. Tim Spencer 10-78

42. Spencer 21-167 and two touchdowns

43. Gary Williams 5-63

44. Keith Byars 15-73

45. Chris Carter 7-172 and one touchdown

46. Keith Byars 23-109

47. John Woolridge, with 25-92

48. Carter, 5-71

49. OSU was the *first* to play in the Rose, Sugar, Cotton, Orange and Fiesta Bowls.

50. Rich Spangler kicked one 52-yard field goal in the 1985 Rose Bowl.

You Could Look It Up—Questions

"Our scouting report didn't tell us anything about him!"
—North Carolina coach after Archie Griffin's record performance in 1972.

FROM THE RECORD BOOK

1. What is the composite record in OSU football history?

2. How many winning seasons has OSU had in its history?

3. How many losing seasons have they had?

4. How many winning seasons in a row has OSU had?

5. How many losing seasons has OSU had in a row?

6. Who was the coach?

7. When was OSU's last losing season?

8. How many .500 seasons has OSU had?

9. What is the school record for the most consecutive losses?

10. What is the school record for the most wins in a row?

INDIVIDUAL RECORDS

11. Who scored the most points in a game?

12. Who scored the most points in a single season?

13. Who scored the most points in a career?

14. Who is the runner-up?

15. What other OSU players have scored more than 200 points in their careers?

16. Who holds the record for the most consecutive games rushing for over 100 yards in a game?

17. Who rushed for the most yards in a game?

18. Who rushed for the most yards in a season?

19. Who rushed for the most yards in a career?

20. Who threw the most touchdown passes in a single game?

21. Who threw the most touchdown passes in a season?

22. Who threw the most touchdown passes in his career?

23. Who is his runner-up?

24. Who passed for the most yards in a game?

25. Who passed for the most yards in a season?

26. Who passed for the most yards in a career?

27. Who is his runner-up?

28. Who threw the most completions in a single game?

29. Who threw the most completions in a season?

30. Who had the most completions in a career?

31. Who is his runner-up?

32. Who threw the most passes in a game?

33. Who threw the most passes in a single season?

34. Who threw the most passes in a career?

35. Who threw the most consecutive passes in a game?

36. Who had the best passing percentage in a season?

37. Who had the best passing percentage in a career?

38. Who is his runner-up?

39. Who caught the most passes in a game?

40. Who caught the most passes in a season?

41. Who caught the most passes in a career?

42. Who is his runner-up?

43. Who caught the most touchdown passes in a game?

44. Who caught the most touchdown passes in a single season?

45. Who caught the most touchdown passes in a career?

46. Who is his runner-up?

47. Who holds the record for the most consecutive games in which he caught a pass?

48. Who holds the record for the most consecutive games in which he caught a pass in a season?

49. Who holds the record for the most consecutive games in which he caught a pass in a career?

50. Who returned the most kick-offs in a season?

51. Who returned the most kick-offs in a career?

52. Who had the most yards returning kick-offs in a season?

53. Who had the most career yards in returning kicks?

54. Who scored the most touchdowns in his OSU career on kick-offs?

55. Who returned the most punts in a season?

56. Who returned the most punts in a career?

57. Who kicked the longest field goal in OSU history?

58. Who is his runner-up?

59. Who kicked the most field goals in his OSU career?

60. Who kicked the most field goals in a season?

61. Who kicked the most field goals in a game?

62. Who holds the record for the most extra points in a season?

63. Who holds the record for the most extra points in a career?

64. Which kicker holds the school record for the most points scored in a career?

65. Who made the most punts in a single game?

66. Who kicked the most extra points in a row?

67. Who had the best career punting average in OSU history?

68. Who is the runner-up?

69. Who is the OSU leader in total offense in a season?

70. Who is the OSU leader in total offense in a game?

71. Who is the OSU leader in total offense in a career?

72. Who holds the OSU record for solo unassisted tackles in a game?

73. Who holds the OSU record for solo unassisted tackles in a season?

74. Who holds the OSU record for solo unassisted tackles in a career?

75.   Who holds the record for the most assisted tackles in a game?

76.   Who has the record for the most assisted tackles in a season?

77.   Who has the record for the most assisted tackles in a career?

78.   Who had the most total tackles in a season?

79.   Who had the most total tackles in a career?

80.   Who is the runner-up?

TEAM RECORDS

81.   What are the most passes attempted by an OSU team in a game?

82.   What are the most passes attempted by an OSU team in a season?

83.   What are the most passes completed by an OSU team in a game?

84.   What are the most passes completed by an OSU team in a season?

85.   In the entire history of OSU, what are the fewest points scored against OSU in a season?

        a. Under 10 b. 11-25 c. Under one-hundred but more than fifty d. Over a hundred

86. What are the most touchdowns scored by OSU in a game?

87. What are the most touchdowns scored by OSU in a season?

88. What are the most rushing yards by an OSU team in a game?

89. What are the most rushing yards by an OSU team in a season?

90. What are the most passing yards by an OSU team in a single game?

91. What are the most passing yards by an OSU team in a season?

92. What were the most points scored by OSU in a game?

93. What were the most points scored by OSU in a season?

    a. Under one-hundred points b. Between 101-200 c. Between 301-400 d. Over 400

94. How many points has OSU scored in its history?

    a. Over 15,000 b. Over 15,000 but fewer than 17,500 c. Between 17,501 and 19,000 d. Over 19,000

95. What are the most points scored against OSU in a game?

96. What are the most points scored against OSU in a season?

    a. Under one-hundred b. Between 101 and 200 c. Between 201-300 d. Over 300

97. What are the most points scored against OSU in its history?

    a. Under 8,000 b. Between 8,001 and 9,000 c. Under 10,000 but more than 9,000 d. Over 10,000

SUPERLATIVE PLAYS IN OSU HISTORY

98. What is the longest run from scrimmage in OSU history?

99. What is the longest touchdown run from scrimmage in OSU history?

100. What is the longest pass play in OSU history?

101. What is the longest pass and lateral play in OSU history?

102. What is the longest non-scoring pass in OSU history?

103. What is the longest punt in OSU history?

104. What is the longest punt return in OSU history?

105. What is the longest kick-off return in OSU history?

THE DISLOYAL OPPOSITION

106. What was the longest run ever made against OSU?

107. Who threw the longest touchdown pass against OSU?

108. Who kicked the longest field goal against OSU?

109. Who made the longest punt in an OSU game?

110. What was the longest punt return against OSU in its history?

111. Who returned a blocked field goal for 110 yards against OSU?

112. Who returned an interception the longest distance for a touchdown against OSU?

ATTENDANCE

113. When was the only year that OSU played before more than a million people?

114. In which year did OSU enjoy its best home game average?

115. In which year did OSU enjoy its largest home attendance?

116. What was the largest crowd to see OSU play anywhere?

a. 95,000 b. 100,000 c. 106,000 d. 110,000

117. What was the largest crowd to see OSU play at home?

a. 75,000 b. 80,000 c. 85,000 d. 90,000

118. What was the largest crowd to see them play in a conference game?

a. 95,000 b. 100,000 c. 106,000 d. 110,000

119. What was the fewest number of people to see OSU play?(Game average for a season)

a. Under 10,000 b. Under 20,000 but more than 10,000 c. Under 30,000 but more than 20,000 d. Over 30,000

Answers

1.   614-243-49

2.   Eighty

3.   Eleven

4.   Twenty-one, and it is still current.

5.   Three (1922-24)

6.   Dr. John Wilce

7.   1966 under Woody Hayes

8.   Five—the last week in 1940 under Frank Schmidt (4-4)

9.   Five, twice (1890-91; 1897)

10. Twenty-four (1972-75)

INDIVIDUAL RECORDS

11. Pete Johnson and Keith Byars (30)

12. Johnson—1975 (156)

13. Johnson—1973-76 (348)

14. Byars—1982-85 (300)

15. Tim Spencer (224), Hopalong Cassady (222), Harold Henson (216), Art Schlichter (210), Jim Otis (210) and Chic Harley (201)

16. Archie Griffin (31)

17. Byars (274) against Illinois in 1984

18. Byars (1,764) in 1984

19. Griffin—1972-75 (5,589)

20. John Borton (5) against Washington State in 1952

21. Jim Karsatos (19)

22. Schlichter (50)

23. Karsatos (36)

24. Schlichter (458) against Florida State in 1981

25. Schlichter (2,551) in 1981

26.   Schlichter—1978-81 (7,547)

27.   Mike Tomczak—1981-84 (5,569)

28.   Schlichter (31), against Florida State in 1981

29.   Schlichter (183) in 1981

30.   Schlichter—1978-81 (497)

31.   Tomczak, 1981-84

32.   Schlichter (52), against Florida State in 1981

33.   Schlichter (350) in 1981

34.   Schlichter—1978-81 (951)

35.   Karsatos (12), against Wisconsin in 1985

36.   Karsatos (.612) in 1985

37.   Karsatos (.571) in 1983-86

38.   John Borton (.569) 1952-54

39.   Gary Williams (13), against Florida State in 1981

40.   Chris Carter (69) in 1986

41.   Carter—1984-86 (168)

42.   Williams—1979-82 (154)

43.   Bob Grimes (4) against Washington State in 1952

44.   Carter (11) in 1986

45.   Carter—1984-86 (27)

46.   Williams—1979-82 and Doug Donley—1977-80 (16)

47.   Williams—1979-82 (48)

48.   Mike Sensibaugh—1959 and Craig Cassady—1975 (9)

49.   Sensibaugh—1968-70 (22)

50.   Jamie Holland—1986 (24)

51.   Hopalong Cassady—1952-55 (42)

52.   Holland—1986 (503)

53.   Cassady—1952-55 (984)

54.   Lenny Willis—1974-75 (2)

55.   Neal Colzie—1973 (40) and Garcia Lane—1982 (40)

56.   Garcia Lane (89) in 1982

57.   Tom Skaldany (59 yards) at Illinois in 1975

58.   Gary Cairns (55 yards) at Illinois in 1966

59.   Valde Janakievski—1977-80 (41)

60.   Janakievski (18) in 1979

You Could Look It Up—Answers

61.   Bob Atha (5) at Indiana in 1981

62.   Rich Spengler (53) in 1983

63.   Spangler—1982-85 (177)

64.   Janakievski (295)

65.   Vic Janowicz (21) in 1950

66.   Janakievski (47) 44 in 1977 and 3 in 1978

67.   Tom Tupa—1984-87 (43.7)

68.   Tom Skaldany (427)

69.   Art Schlichter (2,509) in 1981

70.   Schlichter (412) against Florida State in 1981
       (Included a -46 yards rushing)

71.   Schlichter—1978-81 (8,850)

72.   Tom Cousineau (16) in 1978

73.   Chris Spielman (105) in 1986

74.   Cousineau—1975-78 (259)

75.   Cousineau (20) in 1978

76.   Cousineau (110) in 1978

77.   Marcus Marek—1979-82 (316)

78.   Cousineau (211) in 1978

79.   Marek—1979-82 (572)

80.   Cousineau—1975-78 (569)

TEAM RECORDS:

81.   (52)—Florida State in 1981

82.   (371) in 1981

83.   (31) against Florida State in 1981

84.   (193) in 1981 (.520)

85.   a. Five in 1899

86.   (19) against Oberlin in 1916

87.   (59) in 1974

88.   Twice, (517) against Illinois in 1962 and 1974

89.   (4,199) in 1974

90.   (458) against Florida State in 1981

91.   (2,699)—1981 in twelve games

92.   (128) against Oberlin in 1916 (128-0)

93.   d. (437) in 1974

94.   d. (19,412) 1890-1987

95.   (86) by Michigan in 1902 (86-0)

96.   b. (253) in 1981

97.   b. (9,496) 1890-1987

SUPERLATIVE PLAYS IN OSU HISTORY:

98.   Gene Fekette (89) in 1942 versus Pittsburgh

99.   (88) Morris Bradshaw in 1971 versus Wisconsin

100.   86-yard touchdown, Schlichter against Washington State in 1981

101.   95 yards—Nick Buonamici (73) lateral to Ray Griffin (22 yards) touchdown at Indiana in 1976

102.   75 yards—Jim Karsatos versus Northwestern in 1985

103.   87 yards—Karl Edlund in 1983 against Illinois

104.   87 yards—Bob Demmel of Iowa in 1950 (touchdown)

105.   103 yards—Dean Sensanbaugher (touchdown) in 1943

THE DISLOYAL OPPOSITION:

106.   91 yards by Larry Ferguson of Iowa in 1960 (touchdown)

107.   90 yards by Mike Taliaferro of Illinois in 1962

108.   63 yards by Morton Anderson of Michigan State in 1981

109.   86 yards by Dwight Eddleman of Illinois in 1948

110.   98 yards by Stan Brown of Purdue (touchdown) in 1969

111.   Al Barlow of Michigan in 1905 (touchdown)

112.   98 yards by Julius Rykovich against Illinois in 1946 (touchdown)

ATTENDANCE:

113.   1975—1,010,755 people

114.   1970—89,757 for six games

115.   1982—623,042 for seven games

116.   c. 106,869 in the 1973 Rose Bowl

117.   d. 90,674 against Michigan in 1986

118.   c. 106,255 at Ann Arbor, November 17, 1979

119.   c. 22,743 in 1932

The Big Ten and Other Top Opponents

"It was a great game, one which has unquestionably put Ohio State on the football map!"
—Newspaperman Walter Eckersall after OSU's 14-13 defeat of Wisconsin in 1916.

1. What is OSU's composite record in the Big Ten?

2. Who is the only team that holds an edge over OSU?

3. When did OSU win its first Michigan game?

4. After how many straight losses was this?

5. Which is the only Big Ten team to have joined the Conference after OSU?

The Big Ten and Other Top Opponents—Questions

6. When did OSU first join the Big Ten?

7. How many conference championships has OSU won?

8. How many has it shared?

9. Which is the only team that has won or shared in more Big Ten titles than OSU?

10. What are the most consecutive conference wins?

11. Next to Michigan, which team has won the most against OSU in the Big Ten?

12. What is OSU's record versus Iowa?

13. What is OSU's record versus Indiana?

14. What is OSU's record versus Minnesota?

15. What is OSU's record versus Michigan State?

16. What is OSU's record versus Purdue?

17. What is OSU's record versus Wisconsin?

18. What is OSU's record versus Northwestern?

19. What are the most points OSU scored against Michigan in a *single game*?

20. What are the most points OSU scored against Illinois in a *single game*?

21.   What are the most points OSU scored against Purdue in a *single game*?

22.   What are the most points OSU scored against Michigan State in a *single game*?

23.   What are the most points OSU scored against Wisconsin in a *single game*?

24.   What are the most points OSU scored against Minnesota in a *single game*?

25.   What are the most points OSU scored **against Northwestern im)** *single game*?

26.   What are the most points OSU scored against Iowa in a *single game*?

27.   What are the most points OSU scored against Indiana in a *single game*?

28.   What are the most points Michigan scored against OSU in a single game?

29.   What are the most points Michigan State scored against OSU in a single game?

30.   What are the most points Indiana scored against OSU in a single game?

31.   What are the most points Purdue scored against OSU in a single game?

32.   What are the most points Minnesota scored against OSU in a single game?

33.   What are the most points Iowa scored against OSU in a single game?

34.   What are the most points Northwestern scored against OSU in a single game?

35.   What are the most points Illinois scored against OSU in a single game?

36.   What are the most points Wisconsin scored against OSU in a single game?

TOTAL POINTS:

37.   What are the total number of points that OSU has scored against Michigan?

   a. Under 900 b. 900-1,100 c. 1,101-1,300 d. Over 1,300 (Use for questions 37-45)

38.   Minnesota?

39.   Iowa?

40.   Purdue?

41.   Indiana?

42.   Illinois?

43.   Northwestern?

44.   Wisconsin?

45.   Michigan State?

46.   What are the total number of points scored against OSU by Michigan?

       a. Under 500 b. 500-750 c. 751-1,000 d. Over 1,000 (Use for questions 46-54.)

47.   By Minnesota?

48.   By Iowa?

49.   By Purdue?

50.   By Indiana?

51.   By Illinois?

52.   By Northwestern?

53.   By Wisconsin?

54.   By Michigan State?

THE BEST OF THE REST

55.   Outside of the Conference, against which team does OSU hold the best edge in games played?

56.   Against which team does OSU hold the worst edge? (10 games)

57.   What is the OSU record versus USC?

58.   When was the first time they played?

59.   What is the OSU record against Notre Dame?

60. When was the last time they played?

61. Has OSU ever played an Ivy League team?

62. What is their record versus the Ivy League?

63. When was the last time OSU played an Ivy League team?

64. Who won the game?

65. Columbia University is the school with the longest losing streak. What is OSU's record against the Lions?

66. What is OSU's record versus Alabama?

67. When was the last time they played?

68. What was their record with SMU?

69. When was the last time they played?

70. What is OSU's record with Penn State?

71. When was the last time they played?

72. What is OSU's record with Vanderbilt?

73. When was the last time they played?

74. Has OSU ever played the Dayton YMCA in football?

75. What is OSU's record against Clemson?

76. What is OSU's record against Missouri University?

77. What is OSU's record against Oklahoma?

78. When was the last time they played?

79. Has OSU ever played the Orangemen from Syracuse?

80. When was the last time they played?

81. What is OSU's record against West Virginia?

82. When was the last time they played?

THE ZERO BOYS

83. How many times has OSU shut out its opponent in a game?

84. How many times has OSU been shut out by an opponent?

85. Which team has blanked OSU the most?

86. Which team is the runner-up?

87. Which team has OSU shut out the most?

88. Who is the runner-up?

89. Has any Big Ten team failed to shut out OSU at least once?

90. Against which Big Ten teams has OSU had the fewest shutouts?

Answers

1. 325-127-20

2. Michigan with a 46-33-5

3. 1913

4. 0-12-1

5. Michigan State in 1953

6. 1913

7. Fifteen outright

8. Ten

9. Michigan University

10. Seventeen in 1954-56, 1967-69 and 1974-76

11. Illinois with a 21-51-4 record against OSU

12. 32-12-2

13. 50-11-4

14. 25-6

15. 15-9

16. 25-9-2

17. 41-12-4

18. 44-13-1

19. 50 in 1961 and 1968

20. 49 in 1974 and 1980

21. 49 in 1982

22. 54 in 1969

23. 59 in 1979

24. 69 in 1983

25. 70 in 1981

26. 83 in 1950

27. 56 in 1957 and 1983

28. 86 in 1902

29.   32 in 1965

30.   32 in 1951

31.   41 in 1967

32.   35 in 1981

33.   35 in 1960

34.   28 in a 1982 loss

35.   42 in a 1980 loss

36.   34 in a 1941 loss

TOTAL POINTS

37.   b. 931

38.   a. 864

39.   c. 1,134

40.   a. 808

41.   d. 1,489

42.   d. 1,541

43.   d. 1,402

44.   c. 1,232

45.   a. 580

46. d. 1,310

47. a. 373

48. b. 568

49. a. 489

50. b. 552

51. c. 870

52. b. 514

53. b. 594

54. a. 355

THE BEST OF THE REST

55. 14-1-2 against Denison University (1890-1927)

56. 5-6 against Western Reserve University (1891-1934)

57. 9-9

58. 1937

59. 0-2

60. 1935

61. Yes, Cornell, Columbia, Princeton and University of Pennsylvania

62. 5-3-1

63. In 1953 against University of Pennsylvania

64. Won 12-6

65. 2-0 (1925-26)

66. 0-2

67. 1986—OSU lost in the Kickoff Classic

68. 7-1-1

69. 1978

70. 2-6

71. 1980

72. OSU is 3-1 against Vanderbilt.

73. 1933

74. Yes, they played in 1892 with OSU winning 42-4.

75. In a game Woody Hayes would never forget, OSU lost its only game to Clemson in the 1978 Gator Bowl, 17-15.

76. OSU opened several seasons with Mizzou, compiling an 8-1-1 record.

77. OSU has split its two games with the Sooners.

78. 1983

79. OSU is 2-1 with Syracuse.

80. 1980

81. OSU is 4-1 with West Virginia.

82. OSU opened against West Virginia in 1987.

THE ZERO BOYS

83. Ninety-four

84. Fifty-four

85. Michigan with 21

86. Illinois with 12

87. Indiana with 17

88. Illinois with 15

89. Michigan State in 26 games

90. Michigan State and Minnesota (4)

Other Coaches

"Were he alive today, he would be considered way ahead of his time."
—Former Notre Dame coach, Elmer Layden of Francis Schmidt

1. Woody Hayes won the most games at OSU. Who is in second place?

2. What is his record?

3. Which OSU coach had the best winning percentage?

4. Which coach had the most losses?

5. Which coach had the worst winning percentage?

6. Who coached the most games in OSU history?

7. Who is in second place?

8. Who was OSU's first coach?

9. Which coach had three distinct terms as the OSU coach?

10. Who were the only coaches to go undefeated and untied in OSU football history?

11. Which future NFL coach, owner and Hall of Famer was the head coach at OSU?

12. Who was the first OSU coach to win the National Championship?

13. Who was the first coach to win the Coach of the Year at OSU?

14. Who was the best OSU athlete to become head coach at OSU?

15. How many letters did he earn at OSU?

16. What was OSU's record while he was a player?

17. What position did he play?

18. What was his coaching record?

19. Why did he leave OSU?

20. He once ran a fumble back for a touchdown. When did this happen, who won the game and what was the score?

21. He later coached baseball at which Ivy League College?

22. Which professional baseball team gave him a tryout?

23. Which specific branch of the government did he serve during World War II?

24. Who was OSU's most absent-minded coach?

25. Where did he play college football?

26. At what college did his accomplishments make him a legend in his own time?

27. What were the relative points scored/points allowed at this school for his tenure?

28. He and Woody Hayes are the only OSU coaches to have defeated Michigan four years in a row. What was unusual about his four straight Michigan wins?

29. How many seasons did he coach at OSU?

30. What was his record at OSU?

31. How many Big Ten titles did his teams participate in at OSU?

32. How many times did the OSU team shut out teams during his tenure at OSU?

33. What was his record against Michigan?

34. What was the score of his last Michigan game?

35. What was the score of his last game against Minnesota?

36. What was the score of his last game against Illinois?

37. What was the score of his last game against Indiana?

38. What was the score of his last game against Northwestern?

JOHN WILCE

39. What years did Dr. Wilce coach at OSU?

40. What was his overall record at OSU?

41. What team gave him the most trouble?

42. What was his record against Michigan?

43. What was his record against Iowa?

44. What was his record against Purdue?

45. How many points did Purdue score against OSU in these five games?

46.   Against Indiana?

47.   Against Illinois?

PAUL BROWN

48.   What job did Paul Brown leave to come to OSU?

49.   What assistants from his first job joined him at OSU that first season?

50.   What was his record at OSU?

51.   What was the score of his last game against Michigan?

52.   What was his record against Michigan?

53.   When and where was he born?

54.   Who was his first quarterback?

55.   What future Hall of Fame quarterback defeated OSU's future Hall of Fame coach in 1943?

56.   Who was his replacement?

57.   Who was OSU's opponent in Brown's first game and what was the outcome?

58.   Who was the Missouri coach in that upset?

59.   What was the result of his first game with Michigan?

60. What was his overall record in the Big Ten?

61. What was his overall record against North-western?

62. What was his overall record against Wisconsin?

63. What was his overall record against Indiana?

64. What was his overall record against Michigan?

65. What was his overall record against Purdue?

66. Who gave Brown his first loss?

WES FESLER

67. What was Fesler's job before taking over at OSU in 1947?

68. What was his record against Michigan?

69. What was his record against Purdue?

70. What was his record against Indiana?

71. What was his record against Illinois?

72. What was his record against Wisconsin?

73. What was his record against Minnesota?

74. When Felser resigned in 1951, who got the most votes in a newspaper poll to replace him?

75. Who were the runners-up in that 1951 poll?

76. How many votes did Woody Hayes garner?

77. Who was known as the "brain coach" in the fifties and sixties?

EARLE BRUCE

78. What was Earle Bruce's record against Michigan in his nine seasons?

79. How many bowls did Earle Bruce lead OSU to?

80. What was his bowl record?

81. What was his "favorite" record at OSU in his nine seasons?

82. What was Earle Bruce's career record at OSU?

83. How many losing seasons did Earle Bruce have at OSU?

84. What was his only tie at OSU?

85. What was his Big Ten record?

86. Which was the only team that never beat Bruce in the Big Ten?

87. What was his record against Michigan State?

88. What was his record against Illinois?

89. What was his record against Wisconsin?

90. What was his record against Minnesota?

91. What was his record against Indiana?

92. What was his record against Purdue?

93. What was his record against Iowa?

94. What was Bruce's record in the Rose Bowl?

95. Who was the Athletic Director when Earle Bruce was coach?

96. Who called Columbus the "future former home of Earle Bruce"?

97. Who wrote the book, *Earle Bruce: Beyond the Headset*?

98. Where did Bruce play his college ball?

99. What position did he play?

100. In 1986 Bruce's Buckeyes lost their first two games. When was the last time that happened?

101. Why was Bruce fired?

102. Where was his last coaching job before coming to OSU?

103. How close did his first OSU team come to a perfect record?

104. What was his first coaching job?

105. What was his high school record?

106. Where was his first college coaching position?

107. What was his first head-coaching position?

108. What was Earle Bruce's total college coaching record?

109. How many different bowl games did Earle Bruce take OSU to?

110. Who was OSU's only black assistant in 1987?

JOHN COOPER

111. What was John Cooper's record at Arizona State the season before he took the OSU job?

112. How old is he?

113. What defensive alignment does Cooper favor?

114. Where was he born?

115. Does Cooper have any record against Michigan?

116. What university did he play for?

117. Where was his first head-coaching position?

118. At which five other schools was he an assistant?

119. What was his career coaching record?

120. At Arizona State, how many bowl appearances did he make?

Answers

1. Dr. John Wilce, 1913-28

2. 78-33-9 (.687)

3. Carroll Widdoes, 1944-45, 16-2-0 (.889)

4. Hayes with 61

5. David Edwards 1-7-1 in 1897

6. Hayes with 286

7. Wilce with 120

8. Alexander Lilley was 3-2 in 1890.

9. Jack Ryder helped out in 1890 and then came back to coach in 1892-95 and again in 1898.

10. Widdoes in 1944, Wilce in 1916 and Hayes in 1954, and 1968

11. Paul Brown, 1941-43

12. Brown in 1942 with a 9-1 record

13. Carroll Widdoes in 1944

14. Wes Fesler in 1947

15. Nine in three sports (football, basketball and baseball)

16. 14-7-3

17. Fullback, quarterback and end in 1930

18. 21-13-3

19. Could not stand the repeated stress and his teams did not do well against Michigan

20. Against Northwestern in an 18-6 loss in 1930

21. Harvard

22. St. Louis Cardinals in 1931

23. He served in the Office of Strategic Services (OSS), the forerunner of the CIA.

24. Francis Schmidt was the epitome of the "absent-minded professor."

25. Nebraska University

26. University of Tulsa

27. In 1916, 1919 and 1920, Tulsa outscored its opposition 1791-88.

28. They were all shutouts.

29. Seven, from 1934-40

30. 39-16-1 (.705)

31. Two in 1935 and 1939

32. Twenty-five shutouts for Schmidt's OUS teams

33. 4-3

34. OSU lost 40-0.

35. 0-3

36. 6-1

37. 6-1

38. 4-2-1

JOHN WILCE

39. 1913-28

40.   79-33-9

41.   Michigan

42.   4-7, including six losses in a row

43.   1-4

44.   5-0

45.   All five victories were shutouts.

46.   6-2

47.   5-9-1

PAUL BROWN

48.   He came directly from Massillon High School in Ohio.

49.   Hugh McGranahan, Fritz Heisler and Carroll Widdoes

50.   18-8-1

51.   A 45-7 loss.

52.   1-1-1

53.   Norwalk, Ohio on September 7, 1908

54.   Jack Graf

55.   Otto Graham of Northwestern won 13-0.

56. Assistant Coach, Carroll Widdoes

57. Beat Missouri 12-7

58. Don Faurot

59. A 20-20 tie

60. 9-6-1

61. 1-2

62. 3-0

63. 1-1

64. 1-1

65. 2-1

66. After three straight wins to start in 1941, the Buckeyes of Paul Brown lost to Northwestern.

WES FESLER

67. Head Coach at Pitt

68. 0-3-1

69. 0-1

70. 3-1

71. 2-2

72. 3-0

73. 1-1

74. Brown, 2331 out of 2811

75. Actress Lana Turner, and TV stars, Milton Berle and Lassie

76. Zero

77. James Jones, Director of the Tutoring Program at OSU

EARLE BRUCE

78. 5-4

79. Eight

80. 5-3

81. His OSU teams finished with a 9-2 mark four times.

82. 81-26-1

83. None

84. 13-13 with LSU in New Orleans in 1987

85. 49-16

86. Northwestern (8-0)

87. 6-1

88. 7-2

89.   5-3

90.   8-1

91.   8-1

92.   5-2

93.   5-2

94.   0-2

95.   Rick Bay

96.   Columbus mayor, Dana Rinehart

97.   No one!

98.   Ohio State

99.   He was a 155-pound halfback

100. 1894

101. Because he was not flamboyant enough, nor was he a snappy dresser.

102. Iowa State

103. A one-point loss to USC in the Rose Bowl

104. Mansfield High School in Ohio

105. 82-12-3

106. An Assistant at OSU under Woody Hayes

107. University of Tampa

108. 127-60-1

109. Eight

110. Lenny Willis, backfield coach

JOHN COOPER

111. 7-4-1

112. He was fifty-one in 1988.

113. The 5-2

114. Tennessee

115. His team beat Michigan in the 1987 Rose Bowl.

116. Iowa State

117. The University of Tulsa

118. Iowa State, Oregon State, UCLA, KU and the University of Kentucky

119. 82-40-2

120. Three straight

By the Name and Numbers

"I never saw a man make a tackle with a smile on his face."

—Woody Hayes

Match the following players with the numbers they wore for Ohio State. Some numbers may be used more than once. The numbers to be used are: 1, 3, 7, 10, 11, 13, 14, 19, 20, 21, 22, 26, 28, 31, 32, 35 36, 38, 39, 40, 41, 42, 44, 45, 60, 62, 66, 68, 71, 73, 74, 88, 89, 96 and 99

NAMES:

1. John Burton

2. Jim Parker

3. Vlade Janaklowski

4. Cornelius Greene

5. Rex Kern

6. Jack Tatum

7. Mike McCray

8. Archie Griffin

9. Marcus Maros

10. John Hicks

11. Rick Middleton

12. Jim Stillwagon

13. Bobby Watson

14. Matt Snell

15. Jim Otis

16. Harold Henson

17. Gary Williams

18. George Cooper

19. Art Schlichter

20. Tom Tupa

21. Van DeCree

22.   Pete Cusick

23.   Charlie Csuri

24.   Leo Raskowski

25.   Hubert Bobo

26.   Hopalong Cassady

27.   Paul Warfield

28.   Chris Spielman

29.   Vic Janowicz

30.   Les Horvath

31.   William Willis

32.   Robert Momsen

33.   Bob Brugge

34.   Gus Zarnas

35.   Gene Fekete

36.   Eric Kummerow

37.   Mike Sensibaugh

38.   Vince Workman

39.   Neal Colzie

40.   Jack Dugger

41.   Rich Spangler

42.   Dick Van Raaphorst

What is the significance of the following numbers?

43.   0

44.   34

45.   1711

46.   1890

47.   1978

Identify or explain the following nicknames:

48.   The school "Up North"

49.   Howard

50.   Charles

51.   Champ

52.   Blizzard Bowl

53.   "Close the Gates of Mercy"

54.   Wayne

55.   Gypsy

56.   "House that Chic Built"

57.   "Bad Water Game"

58.   Baby Bucks

59.   Supermen

60.   The MOB

61.   "The Toe"

62.   "Best Civilian team in the country"

63.   "The Animal"

WHO SAID THIS?

64.   "The alumni never won a football game in their life!"

65.   "Life with Woody was never 'Easy'!"

66.   "The only trouble I have with my eyes is that my glasses won't stay in place because I've got this peanut nose."

67.   "In Woody Hayes we have a coach...who's got the courage to face the cotton pellets of words and innuendoes and keep on plugging ..."

68.   "I think Rich Bay is the strongest Athletic Director in the Country!"

69.   "I'm not here to defend Earle Bruce, but all I can say is that it makes OSU look bad."

70. "I've never been a Woody Hayes admirer!"

71. "Woody Hayes isn't crazy enough to get committed but *if* he ever does, they'd never let him out!"

72. "For my money, that's the finest team ever put together in college football history."

73. "I think back and remembering who we had on that team and I just can't believe anyone could beat us!"

74. "Got is not dead! He's alive and coaching at OSU!"

Answers

1.	20	11.	32
2.	62	12.	68
3.	13	13.	45
4.	7	14.	41
5.	10	15.	35
6.	32	16.	38
7.	99	17.	44
8.	45	18.	44
9.	36	19.	10
10.	74	20.	19

21.	88	32.	73
22.	71	33.	1
23.	60	34.	26
24.	39	35.	44
25.	42	36.	14
26.	40	37.	3
27.	42	38.	42
28.	36	39.	20
29.	31	40.	96
30.	22	41.	10
31.	89	42.	86

SIGNIFICANCE OF THE FOLLOWING:

43. Number given to the captain pictured in the team photo

44. WOSU-TV that does OSU's football games

45. Woody Hayes's address on Cardiff Road

46. Year OSU football started

47. Year Woody was fired

By the Name and Numbers—Answers

IDENTIFICATIONS:

48.   Michigan

49.   Hopalong Cassady's first name

50.   Chic Harley's first name

51.   Harold Henson's first name (1972-74)

52.   OSU's 9-3 loss to Michigan in a bad snow-storm in 1950

53.   Frank Schmidt's propensity for running up the score

54.   Woody Hayes's first name

55.   Gene Fekete

56.   Ohio Stadium

57.   1942 loss to Wisconsin when several players got sick

58.   1943 Buckeyes

59.   1968-70 Buckeye teams

60.   1985 defensive backfield known as "Men of Brutality"

61.   Lou Groza

62.   The 1944 Buckeyes

63. Harold Henson

WHO SAID THIS?:

64. Woody Hayes

65. AD Dick Larkin

66. Woody Hayes in 1977

67. Jack Fullen, Secretary of the OSU Alumni Association

68. Earle Bruce

69. Bo Schembechler

70. Coach Jack Mollenkept of Purdue in 1956

71. Coach Forest Evashevski of Iowa

72. Wisconsin coach, John Coatta in 1969

73. Jack Tatum

74. Student banner at OSU in the seventies

In for the Money: OSU in the Pros

"This will heal, son, then others will pay!"
—Champ Henson's father to his son after the latter's knee surgery in 1973

Name the *first* professional team the following OSU football players began their careers with.

1. Hopalong Cassady

2. Vic Janowicz

3. Jim Parker

4. John Brockington

5. Chic Harley

6. Rowland Tatum

7. Mark Cousineau

8. Archie Griffin

9. Bobby Watkins

10. Jim Otis

11. Rex Kern

12. Matt Snell

13. Art Schlichter

14. William Willis (1944)

15. Les Horvath

16. Mike Tomczak

17. Pete Johnson

18. Keith Byars

19. Paul Warfield

20. Chris Carter

21. Ron Spring

22. John Hicks

23. Lou Groza

24. Jim Stillwagon

25.　　Bob Ferguson

26.　　Randy Gradishar

27.　　Jack Tatum

28.　　Mike Sensibaugh

29.　　Neal Colzie

30.　　Brian Baschnagel

31.　　Jack Dugger

32.　　Angello Lavelli

33.　　Bob Brudzinski

34.　　Chuck Bryant

35.　　Nick Roman

36.　　John Borton

37.　　Gene Fekete

38.　　Thad Weed

39.　　Jim Straubaugh

40.　　Rufus Mayes

41.　　Ted Provost

42.　　Todd Bell

43.   Dick LeBeau

44.   Leo Hayden

45.   Jim Marshall

46.   Hubert Bobo

47.   Doug Van Horn

48.   Bob Vogel

49.   Bob Watkins

50.   Ollie Cline

Answers

1. Detroit Lions (1956)

2. Washington Redskins (1955)

3. Baltimore Colts (1957)

4. Green Bay Packers (1971)

5. Chicago Bears (1921)

6. Miami Dolphins (1984)

7. Montreal Alouttees CFL (1979)

8. Cincinnati Bengals (1975)

9. Chicago Bears (1955)

10. New Orleans Saints (1970)

11. Baltimore Colts (1971)

12. New York Jets (1964)

13. Baltimore Colts (1981)

14. Cleveland Browns AA (1945)

15. Los Angeles Rams (1947)

16. Chicago Bears (1985)

17. Cincinnati Bengals (1977)

18. Philadelphia Eagles (1982)

19. Cleveland Browns (1964)

20. Philadelphia Eagles (1987)

21. Dallas Cowboys (1979)

22. New York Giants (1973)

23. Cleveland Browns AA (1946)

24. Toronto Argonauts (1970)

25. Pittsburgh Steelers (1962)

26. Denver Broncos (1973)

27. Oakland Raiders (1971)

28. Kansas City Chiefs (1971)

29.   Oakland Raiders (1975)

30.   Chicago Bears (1976)

31.   Buffalo AA (1946)

32.   Cleveland Browns AA (1946)

33.   Los Angeles Rams (1977)

34.   St. Louis Cardinals (1962)

35.   Cincinnati Bengals (1970)

36.   Cleveland Browns (1957)

37.   Cleveland Browns AA (1946)

38.   Pittsburgh Steelers (1955)

39.   Chicago Cardinals (1946)

40.   Chicago Bears (1969)

41.   Minnesota Vikings (1970)

42.   Chicago Bears (1982)

43.   Detroit Lions (1959)

44.   Minnesota Vikings (1971)

45.   Cleveland Browns (1960)

46.   Los Angeles Rams (1960)

47.   Detroit Lions (1966)

48.   Baltimore Colts (1963)

49.   Chicago Bears (1955)

50.   Cleveland Browns (1948)

OSU Oddities and Minutiae

"We have enough Bunnies in Columbus...We don't have to go elsewhere to find them."
　　　　　　　　　　　　—Woody Hayes in 1970

1. What was the score of the best opening game in OSU history?

2. In the last ten years, how many times has OSU finished in the Top Ten?

3. What was the biggest early debate of 1987 on the OSU football team?

4. Who are the Buckeye announcers on TV 34 (1987)?

5. How many temporary seats are there at OSU Stadium?

   a. Under 12,000 b. Between 12,000 and 20,000 c. Between 20,001 and 30,000 d. Over 30,000

6. How much did it cost to build the stadium?

7. What was the occasion for Woody Hayes's last public appearance?

8. Where does the OSU football team stay when they play at Michigan?

9. Where do the Buckeyes play their home games?

10. What was the name of OSU's prior football field?

11. What is the area covered by Ohio Stadium in Columbus?

12. What is the capacity of this stadium?

13. What is the playing surface made of?

14. When did they first play here?

15. How many people have seen OSU play football in its history?

    a. Over 10 million b. Over 20 million c. Over 25 million d. Over 30 million

16. In what year did they play their first game?

17. Who was the opponent and what was the score?

18. Where was that inaugural game played?

19. Who paid for the astroturf at OSU Stadium in 1971?

20. What happened to the sod that was removed from the field?

21. What was the most bizarre use of former OSU sod?

22. What are the school's colors?

23. What was the score of the first OSU-Michigan Game (1897)?

24. How many times did OSU defeat Michigan from 1897-1912?

25. What national magazine did Woody Hayes direct his furor at in 1970?

26. What OSU Athletic Director once replaced Branch Rickey as a college coach?

27. What is the most ties an OSU team has experienced in a season?

28. What is the most famous tie in OSU history?

29. How many times has OSU held its opponents scoreless?

30. How many times have they been held score-less?

31. What was the school's worst loss?

32. When was OSU's first undefeated team?

33. Why was the Michigan game postponed in 1963?

34. When it was finally played what was the score?

35. What was the significance of the crowd that attended?

36. In 1973 which Big Ten team scored the most points on OSU?

37. Which OSU players were first-round selections in the 1973 NFL Draft?

38. Who was the Homecoming Queen for OSU in 1926?

39. Who were the runners-up?

40. What is the school song, played at football games?

41. Who was the first Buckeye chosen in the 1988 NFL Draft?

42. How many Buckeyes were selected in the 1988 NFL Draft?

43.   Which team drafted Tom Tupa?

44.   Which team drafted Chris Spielman?

45.   Who was the last Buckeye chosen in the 1988 NFL Draft?

46.   Which teams selected more than one Buckeye?

47.   Which were the only schools that had more players drafted than OSU?

48.   Name the Big Ten schools that had a player drafted ahead of OSU.

49.   How many different OSU players have become All-Americans?

50.   In which season did OSU have the most All-Americans?

51.   In which season did OSU have four players drafted on the first round?

52.   Who were they?

Answers

1. In 1933, OSU started its season by defeating Virginia University 75-0.

2. Just three times: the most recent a sixth place (UPI) finish in 1986

3. Earle Bruce's game attire during the season

4. Jack Kramer and Paul Warfield

5. a) (11,990)

6. 1,341,000 in 1922

7. At a ceremony honoring Archie Griffin's induction into the National College Football Hall of Fame

8. The Plymouth Hilton

9. Ohio Stadium

10. Ohio Field

11. Ten acres

12. 85,339

13. Astroturf

14. 1922

15. c) 25,665,231 thru 1986

16. May 3, 1890

17. Beat Ohio Wesleyan 20-14

18. At Ohio Wesleyan in Delaware, Ohio, fifteen miles North of Columbus

19. Lou Fischer, a rabid OSU fan paid $380,000 for the rug in 1971.

20. They gave it to their fans.

21. One woman put it on her husband's grave.

22. Gray and Scarlet

23. Michigan won 34-0.

24. Not once—just two ties; 0-0 in 1900 and 3-3 in 1910

25. *Playboy*

26, Dr. L. Wilbur, St. John's

27. Three in 1897, 1910, 1924 and 1932

28. A 10-10 tie with Michigan in 1973

29. 94

30. 54

31. 86-0

32. 1899 (9-0-1)

33. Assassination of President John F. Kennedy

34. OSU won 14-10

35. Smallest in history of Michigan Stadium

36. Iowa with just 13 points

37. John Hicks, Randy Gradishar and Bob Middleton

38. Maudene Ormsby, a 1,000-pound Holstein cow

39. Evangelist Aimee McPherson, Helen of Troy and singer Sophie Tucker

40. "Across the Field"

41. Eric Kumerow

42. Eight

43. Phoenix Cardinals

44. Detroit Lions on the second round

45. Henry Brown was the 277th pick in the tenth round.

46. Detroit and the Miami Dolphins

47. Oklahoma, Michigan and UCLA

48. Michigan

49. Eighty-one

50. Seven in 1974

51. 1971

52. John Brockington (9th), Jack Tatum (19th), Tim Andrews (23rd) and Leo Hayden (25th)

Photographs

1. This coaching staff could only manage a 4-4 record in 1940. Who was the head coach?

2. This player was an All-American tackle in 1944.

3. This player was OSU's first Heisman winner.

4. This coach had a professional team named after him.

5. This coach eventually learned to dress better.
    Who was he and what was the year?

6. In what was called "the great game," OSU was the best team in the country for three quarters. What was the game?

7.   This man did more than hand off to Cassady.

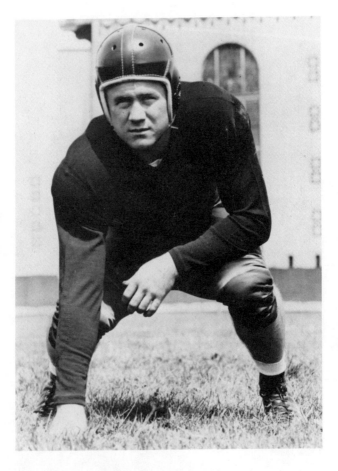

8. This player was an All-American guard in 1942.

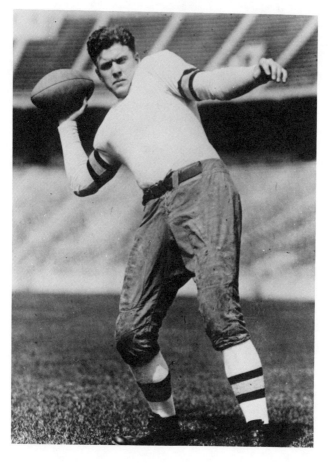

9. As a coach he couldn't beat Michigan, so Woody followed.

10. Which team did Hopalong badger with this run?

11. This "gypsy" finished third in the Heisman voting in 1942.

12. They called him "Champ."

13. This back later found a home in St. Louis.

14. While Archie won the Heisman, he won the Big Ten's silver football in 1975.

15. The only punter in OSU history to be named an All-American.

16.   He was called the "assassin."

17. He was Woody's choice for captain in 1973.

18. He later caught for the Pittsburgh Pirates.

19.   His speed took him to Canton, Ohio.

20. He had to sit while Otis played.

21.   He picked off the most passes in OSU history.

22. He won the Lombardi award in 1970.

23. He had twin Heismans.

24. When did this stadium open to the public?

Answers

1. Francis Schmidt (third from left)

2. William Willis

3. Les Horvath

4. Paul Brown

5. Woody Hayes, 1951

6. OSU's 1935 18-13 loss to Notre Dame

7. Quarterback John Borton

8. Lindell Houston

9. Wes Fesler

10. Wisconsin

11. Gene Fekete

12. Harold Henson

13. Jim Otis

14. Cornelius Greene

15. Tom Skaldany

16. Jack Tatum

17. John Hicks

18. Vic Janowicz

19. Paul Warfield

20. John Brockington

21. Mike Sensibaugh

22. Jim Stillwagon

23. Archie Griffin

24. August 3, 1921